Targeting Comprehension

Year 3

Peter Alford and Aimee Bloom

PASCAL

Targeting Comprehension Year 3

Copyright © 2020 Blake Education
Reprinted 2021, 2022, 2025
ISBN 978 1 925490 62 6

Published by Pascal Press
PO Box 250
Glebe NSW 2037
contact@pascalpress.com.au

Authors: Peter Alford and Aimee Bloom
Publisher: Lynn Dickinson
Editor: Marie Theodore
Typesetter: Stacey Grainger
Series consultant: Del Merrick
Printed by Wai Man Book Binding (China) Ltd

Reproduction and communication for educational purposes
The Australian *Copyright Act 1968* (the Act) allows a maximum of one chapter or 10% of the pages of this work, whichever is the greater, to be reproduced and/or communicated by any educational institution for its educational purposes provided that the educational institution (or that body that administers it) has given a remuneration notice to the Copyright Agency under the Act.
For details of the licence for educational institutions contact:
Copyright Agency
Level 12, 66 Goulburn Street
Sydney, NSW 2000
Tel: (02) 9394 7600
Fax: (02) 9394 7601
E-mail: memberservices@copyright.com.au

Reproduction and communication for other purposes
Except as permitted under the Act (for example, a fair dealing for the purpose of study, research, criticism or review) no part of this book may be reproduced, stored in a retrieval system, communicated or transmitted in any form or by any means without prior written permission. All inquiries should be made to the publisher at the address above.

ACARA ENGLISH CURRICULUM CORRELATIONS
All material identified by AC | Australian CURRICULUM is material subject to copyright under the Australian Copyright Act 1968 (Cth) and is owned by the Australian Curriculum, Assessment and Reporting Authority 2017. For all Australian Curriculum material, this is an extract from the Australian Curriculum.

Disclaimer: ACARA neither endorses nor verifies the accuracy of the information provided and accepts no responsibility for incomplete or inaccurate information. In particular, ACARA does not endorse or verify that:
- The content descriptions are solely for a particular year and subject;
- All the content descriptions for that year and subject have been used; and
- The author's material aligns with the Australian Curriculum content descriptions for the relevant year and subject.

You can find the unaltered and most up-to-date version of the material at http://www.australiancurriculum.edu.au.
This material is reproduced with the permission of ACARA.

AUSTRALIAN CURRICULUM CORRELATIONS: English

YEAR THREE

Analysing, interpreting and evaluating
AC9E3LY03 identify the audience and purpose of imaginative, informative and persuasive texts through their use of language features and/or images
AC9E3LY05 use comprehension strategies when listening and viewing to build literal and inferred meaning, and begin to evaluate texts by drawing on a growing knowledge of context, text structures and language features

Examining Literature
AC9E3LE03 discuss how an author uses language and illustrations to portray characters and settings in texts, and explore how the settings and events influence the mood of the narrative

Contents

HOW TO USE THIS BOOK

A good understanding of comprehension is essential for effective writing and communication. This book gives you the skills to unpick texts so that you can understand all the meanings embedded in them. It contains activities for both Literal and Inferential comprehension. In other words — it teaches you to read and understand what is stated in the text and how to read between the lines.

Literal comprehension is simply understanding exactly what the text says, the information and facts directly stated in the text.

Inferential comprehension is more complicated. It requires you to interpret ideas, intent or information in the text and to make assumptions.

Inferential comprehension can be divided into the following elements:

- **Inferring** – making assumptions based on context
- **Predicting** – imagining where aspects of a text may lead
- **Analysing** – interpreting the ideas behind what is written
- **Making connections** – finding links between two elements of a text
- **Critical reflection** – drawing on your own experience and knowledge to understand characters

Each of these elements has its own section in this book, as does literal comprehension. They are explained using a variety of informative, imaginative and persuasive sample texts.

Also included is an assessment section for each of the five comprehension elements and removable answers. Australian Curriculum correlations can be found on page ii.

Quick Guide to:

• LITERAL COMPREHENSION •

Franklin, the dog, bounded up the hill, through the tall, green grass. His owner, Ali, ran quickly behind him.

"Look at that view!" Ali exclaimed. "I've never seen a more beautiful sunset."

Ali sighed happily and sat on the grass. Franklin looked at Ali, before running in little circles and sniffing the grass. Finally finding what he was looking for, Franklin proudly bounced over to his owner with a stick in his mouth.

"I don't know where you get all your energy from!" laughed Ali. "OK, let's play fetch again."

Answering questions about text often means finding the answer in what you have read. Sometimes you are asked to remember what was in the text. These are **literal** questions.

Example of a literal question:
In the sample text above, the story is about a dog and his owner running and playing together. What did Franklin find in the grass?

Answer: Franklin sniffed around and found a stick in the grass.

Answers to **literal questions** are always facts from the text and there is always one correct answer in the text. The correct answer can always be seen in the text and can be thought of as 'right-there' or 'on-the-page' information.

Example of a literal question:
In the text above, Ali thought the view was beautiful. What was she looking at that made her say that?

Answer: Ali was looking at the beautiful sunset.

DID YOU NOTICE?

The answer to the question can be found directly in the text. You don't guess (or infer) what the answer might be, as the answer is in the story.

LITERAL

"Improving your surfing skills is no small feat," Harper thought to herself. "I've just got to keep trying."

Harper lay on her surfboard and propped herself up so she could see the waves rippling toward her. "This time for sure," she said to herself. "I've got this!"

As the waves grew ever closer, Harper readied herself. With feet dangling over the edge of the surfboard and her body lying flat on the waxy surface of the board, she began to paddle. "Go! Go! Go!" Harper thought.

Harper jumped to her feet as the surfboard gained speed, stretching her arms to the side to balance. However, as she surfed down the face of the wave, Harper felt off balance as if the surfboard was tipping her off. Falling over the front of the board, she tumbled about under the water as the wave passed overhead.

Scrambling for the surface, Harper grabbed her surfboard, draping her arms over the top so she could float for a moment and catch her breath. Shaking the salt out of her eyes, Harper set her jaw and her eyes glinted with determination. "This time for sure," she repeated.

1 What is Harper learning to do? Tick the correct answer. Harper is learning to ...

a) snowboard. ☐

b) surf. ☐

c) skateboard. ☐

TARGETING COMPREHENSION 3 © PASCAL PRESS ISBN 9781925490626

LITERAL

2 Colour all the verbs (action words) mentioned in the story.

lay	swam	surfed
kicked	jumped	tumbled
ran	grabbed	cried

3 What did Harper do to be able to catch a wave? Number the steps in the correct order from 1 to 4.

a) jump to her feet ☐
b) paddle ☐
c) stretch her arms to the side ☐
d) lie on the board ☐

4 True or False? Harper fell off the back of her surfboard.

☐ True ☐ False

5 Immediately after Harper fell off her board she did a few things. Write what actions she did.

____

____

____

____

____

6 Harper set her ______________ and her ______________ glinted with determination. "This time for ______________," she repeated.

Have you ever thought about why we have day and night? It's not just because animals and people need to sleep — it all has to do with the relationship between the sun and the Earth.

The sun is at the centre of our solar system. Even though it looks like the sun is moving across the sky, it actually stays in the same position, shining light on the Earth.

The reason why we can't see this light all the time is because the Earth spins like a top. In scientific terms, this is called rotating on an axis. Every day the Earth makes one complete rotation on its axis.

Night-time occurs when the Earth has rotated far enough that we can't see the sun anymore. However, the sun is still shining — we just can't see it from where we are.

Did you know?

At any given time, the light from the sun shines on half of the Earth!

1 True or False? The sun moves across the sky during the day.

☐ True ☐ False

2 Why do we have night-time? Tick the correct answer.

a) so that we know it's time to sleep ☐

b) because animals can't sleep during the day ☐

c) because the Earth has rotated, and we can't see the sun ☐

d) because the sun has moved away from the Earth ☐

3 Read the text and find the missing words.

The Earth ______________ like a top, which is called ______________ on an ______________.

TARGETING COMPREHENSION 3 © PASCAL PRESS ISBN 9781925490626

LITERAL

4 How long does it take for the Earth to make one full rotation?

____

5 If the sun never stops shining, why can't we always see it?

____

____

____

6 Draw and label a diagram showing the relationship between the sun and the Earth. Use shading or colours to show where the sun is shining on the Earth.

Often, we don't get things right straightaway. Learning and creating new things takes time and practice — especially if it's something tricky. However, it's important not to give up if we fail or find things hard. We will only achieve our goal if we keep trying.

Thomas Edison was a scientist who is famous for inventing the light bulb. However, he didn't come across the perfect design the first time he tried. In fact, Thomas Edison did almost 3000 different experiments before discovering one design that worked! During his lifetime he also patented over 1000 different inventions. Can you imagine trying something 3000 times before getting it right?

Dr Seuss, author of books like *The Cat in the Hat* and *Green Eggs and Ham*, had his first book rejected 27 times before one company decided they wanted to print it. He then went on to sell over 600 million books! Can you imagine asking 27 different people whether they liked what you had written before someone said, "Yes"?

Michael Jordan is one of the most famous basketball players of all time. However, when he was in high school, he got kicked out of his school basketball team. Michael Jordan didn't let this discourage him from playing and he later became world famous because of his basketball skills. Can you imagine getting kicked off a school team but later becoming world famous at that sport because you didn't give up?

So next time you get an answer wrong or you miss a goal, remind yourself of these three people and think about the amazing things you could achieve if you just keep trying.

1 Who was famous for inventing the light bulb? Tick the correct answer.

a) Dr Seuss ☐

b) Michael Jordan ☐

c) Thomas Edison ☐

d) The Cat in the Hat ☐

TARGETING COMPREHENSION 3 © PASCAL PRESS ISBN 9781925490626

LITERAL

2 How many times did Thomas Edison's experiments fail before he experienced success? ______________

3 ______________ companies told Dr Seuss they didn't want to publish his book.

4 True or False? Michael Jordan became world famous for the same sport that kicked him off the team in high school.

☐ True ☐ False

5 Match each verb (action word) with one Thing Noun and one Person Noun from the text. Colour the boxes to show your matches. Each group of matching words should be the same colour.

Verb	Thing Nouns	Person Nouns
experiment	sport	Dr Seuss
practice	book	Thomas Edison
ask	invention	Michael Jordan

6 Why shouldn't we give up if we fail at something the first time?

____

____

____

Quick Guide to:

INFERRING

The four killers surrounded Bertie who had built up some speed in fear for his life. Gnar got closer and closer followed by the biggest killer of the pod. They opened their mouths, showing their sharp pointed teeth. Gnar suddenly changed direction and torpedoed in at Bertie's flipper. Bertie swung his mighty tail and smacked the killer across the face, knocking him out of the water. He landed many metres away.

Answering questions about text often means finding the answer in what you have read. Sometimes you are asked to remember what was in the text. These are **literal** questions.

Example of a literal question:
In the sample text above, the story tells about a whale fighting for his life. How did the whale protect himself?

Answer: Whales have a mighty tail and the whale swung this at the killers.

Unlike literal questions, when you **infer**, the answers are not in the text. You have to guess the answer by using information in the text. **Inferring** is guessing, using what you already know.

Example of an inferring question:
What the 'killers' are, is not explained in the text. What do you think they are? What words helped you to guess your answer?

Answer: The 'killers' were killer whales because the text used the word 'pod'. Pod is the word for a group of whales.

DID YOU NOTICE?

The answer to the question is not in the text. You have to look for clues to **infer (guess)** the answer by using the words. To do this, you need to know about the word 'pod'. Pod is the name of a group of whales, therefore the 'killers' are killer whales.

TARGETING COMPREHENSION 3 © PASCAL PRESS ISBN 9781925490626

INFERRING

The ship pitched over the top of the next wave as lightning flashed overhead. “We have to steer her into the wind,” yelled the captain, “otherwise we’ll crash on those rocks.”

The captain pointed through the rain to some rocks in the distance and the first mate jumped into action. “Hoist that sail!” he yelled, his voice struggling to be heard above the wind. “Faster! Faster!”

Slipping on the wet deck, the crew pulled the ropes with all their might. As the sail began to rise, the captain continued to try to steer the ship on course.

“Are we going to make it?” the first mate yelled, but the wind whipped away his words and the captain didn’t hear him. The first mate turned back to face the crew. “Pull!” he shouted.

The ship leaned to one side as the wind filled the sails. “It’s going to be close!” roared the captain. “Hold on!” The crew grabbed whatever they could, the mast, the ropes, the side of the ship, as they sailed ever closer toward the jagged rocks.

The ship sailed over the crest of another wave and the crew could see the rocks beside them. Water from the waves crashed onto the deck and the rain-soaked crew struggled to hold onto the ship. “We’re not going to make it!” cried one of the crew.

“We will! We will!” a crewmate replied.

As the ship rounded the corner, hugging the coastline, the crew began to cheer. “Well done!” the first mate told the captain.

“Well done,” the captain replied. “We live to sail another day.”

Was this good weather for sailing? What makes you say that?

____

____

____

INFERRING

2 Why were the crew slipping on the deck of the ship? Tick the correct answer.

a) The deck of the ship was wet from the rain. ☐

b) The deck of the ship was wet because someone spilled a drink. ☐

c) The crew were all wearing slippery shoes. ☐

3 Why couldn't the captain hear the first mate? Tick the correct answer.

a) The captain didn't have very good hearing. ☐

b) The wind was too noisy and made it hard to hear anyone. ☐

c) The first mate was speaking too softly. ☐

4 Why did the captain tell the crew to hang on?

____

____

____

5 Tick the reasons why it might have been difficult for the crew to hang onto the ship.

☐ rain	☐ ropes	☐ waves
☐ lightning	☐ wind	☐ thunder

6 Why did the crew begin to cheer? Colour the correct answer.

a) The storm was over. ⚓

b) The wind died down. ⚓

c) They didn't crash into the rocks. ⚓

TARGETING COMPREHENSION 3 © PASCAL PRESS ISBN 9781925490626

INFERRING

These may look like plastic bags floating past, but they're actually jellyfish! The Venus comb girdle is like a long see-through ribbon. It can grow to almost 1.5 metres long, but is only about 8 centimetres wide.

Source: *That's Bizarre*, Pascal Press. [abridged]

1 Why do you think this jellyfish is see-through rather than coloured? Tick the box that gives the best reason.

a) It has no colour so it is not tasty for fish to eat. ☐

b) It is see-through so it's able to move through the water faster. ☐

c) It's see-through so that fish can't see it very well and it won't get eaten. ☐

d) It's not coloured because it wants to look like a plastic bag. ☐

2 Every year thousands of fish and dolphins die because they swallow clear plastic bags. Why do you think fish and dolphins mistake plastic bags for jellyfish?

____

____

____

3 What could we do to stop fish and dolphins eating plastic bags and then dying? Colour the best statement.

a) We should make brightly coloured bags. ☐

b) We should stop using plastic bags and put all rubbish in the bin. ☐

c) We should make bags that dissolve in sea water. ☐

INFERRING

Some geckos (lizards) are masters of disguise.
They are kitted out with rough skin, a flat body
and a tail that looks like something from a tree.
They blend in seamlessly on bark, leaves and rocks.
These geckos also have clawed feet like a bird,
unlike the sticky pads other geckos have.

Source: *That's Bizarre*, Pascal Press. [abridged]

4 Can you guess what part of a tree the gecko's tail may look like? What is the reason for this shape?

____

____

____

____

5 What colours would this gecko be? Colour the shape of the best statement.

a) The gecko is the colour of the leaves on the ground and the bark of the trees where it lives. △

b) Bright purple and red skin helps to make birds think that the gecko may be bad to eat. □

c) The gecko is bright orange because it needs to find a female as a mate. ◇

d) The gecko has a leaf-shaped tail. ○

6 Geckos which live inside houses have sticky pads on their feet but this gecko has claws. Why do you think they have claws?

____

____

____

____

TARGETING COMPREHENSION 3 © PASCAL PRESS ISBN 9781925490626

INFERRING

Many plants and insects help each other. When an insect takes a drop of nectar from a plant, the insect gets pollen on its body. Some of this pollen brushes off on to the next plant the insect visits. This helps the plant to grow new seeds. In fact, if we didn't have insects, we may all starve.

Source: Brainwaves, *Plants That Bite Back*, Blake Education.

INSECTS ARE NOT THE ENEMY

Insects can be annoying, but please DON'T kill them! Without them, we could all PERISH. Some insects help to spread pollen and we COULDN'T survive without them. Plants wouldn't be able to make seeds without the help of insects. And without bees, we WOULDN'T have any honey! NO insects, **NO FOOD!!!**

1 Read the main points and decide which one matches the reading texts. Tick one box.

Insects are useful because ...

a) they are able to help us keep flowers under control. ☐

b) many people have jobs getting rid of insects. ☐

c) without them, plants would have one less way of spreading pollen and making seeds and fruit. ☐

d) they spread honey from plant to plant. ☐

Pitcher Plants

Insects that explore the pitcher plant are not so lucky. An insect comes over to taste the nectar. One slip and it falls down the pitcher plant's slippery slope and is trapped. The insect drowns in a pool of juices. It is now a meal for the plant.

Source: Brainwaves, *Plants That Bite Back*, Blake Education.

INFERRING

2 What is the main idea of the information text about the pitcher plant on page 13?

____

____

____

PITCHER PLANTS – NATURE'S WONDER INSECT KILLERS

You **must** have a pitcher plant in your house! Just imagine not having to spray for insects! The good old pitcher plant gobbles up insects! This little wonder should be in every home. No more insect sprays which are highly poisonous and perhaps a danger! You shouldn't be without this useful plant!

3 The two texts about pitcher plants have similar information. One has facts and the other is trying to persuade you to do something. What is the persuasive text trying to get you to do?

____

____

____

4 After reading the two texts about pitcher plants, choose one statement which is correct. Tick the box.

a) Pitcher plants are useful because they spray poison. ☐

b) Pitcher plants kill insects and help us control these creatures. ☐

c) You must get a pitcher plant because it's delicious to eat. ☐

d) No house should be without a pitcher plant as they are smelly. ☐

e) Pitcher plants may eat humans, beware! ☐

TARGETING COMPREHENSION 3 © PASCAL PRESS ISBN 9781925490626

Quick Guide to:

PREDICTING

Stone fish live on the bottom of reefs in the north of Australia. They don't move around much, lying amongst rocks and sand on the sea floor. They wait for dinner to just swim on by. Having long spines saves stone fish from being on the favourite food list of every creature in the ocean, as well as fishermen. The pain of a sting from these fish is said to drive humans crazy.

Tina's mum had told her about these terrible fish and she always wore shoes in shallow water. The fisherman who had just come to the beach walked straight into the water with nothing on his feet.

PREDICTING

Answering questions about text often means finding the answer in what you have read. Sometimes you are asked to remember what was in the text. These are **literal** questions.

Example of a literal question:
Stone fish lie on the ocean floor. Where do stone fish live in Australia?

Answer: Stone fish are found in the north of Australia.

Unlike literal questions, when you **predict**, the answer is not in the text. **Predicting** is guessing what happens next or may happen in the text using what you have already read and understood.

Example of a predicting question:
Predict what may happen next to the man in the story.

Answer: The man who has bare feet may step on a stone fish and need to go to hospital.

DID YOU NOTICE?

Predicting is another type of inferring. Inferring is a bit like predicting because the answers are not found in the text. To answer these questions, you have to think about the text you have read and use what you know to guess the answers. Predicting questions are about what **hasn't happened yet** in the text.

PREDICTING

"Jump. Come on ... I dare you ... Jump!"

I was perched on the garage roof at Owen's place. Owen and Nick were standing on the path below me.

"Come on, Nathan," said Owen. "We haven't got all day."

"OK ...OK ..." I said and had another look over the edge. It was summer holidays and we had been playing ...

Source: Sparklers, *The Zipper*, Blake Education. [abridged]

1 What do you think Nathan is thinking about doing? Tick one of the boxes.

a) Nathan is going to eat his morning tea on the roof. ☐

b) Nathan is thinking whether he should jump off the roof. ☐

c) He is thinking about how much fun he's been having over the holidays. ☐

d) Nathan is thinking about how the garage roof needs to be cleaned. ☐

2 Why do you think Nathan went onto the roof? Write your answer in a sentence and explain why you think this.

____

____

____

____

3 What game do you think the boys have been playing at this time of year? Write your answer in a sentence and explain why you think this.

____

____

____

____

TARGETING COMPREHENSION 3 © PASCAL PRESS ISBN 9781925490626

The path below was made of concrete. Owen had jumped down from here last week for a dare. "Are you scared, or what?"

"No," I answered. Owen did a pretend yawn, a very loud one. He turned to Nick. "He's going to be up there all day. Let's go and watch TV."

"Wait," I said. "Don't go ..."

Source: Sparklers, *The Zipper*, Blake Education. [abridged]

PREDICTING

Can you predict what happens next in the story? Shade the arrow which best fits what happens next.

 a) Owen fell asleep after his pretend yawn.

 b) Nathan put on his Superman cape.

 c) Nathan thought about how Owen had jumped and he did the same.

"Ooo ..." I moaned.

"Are you all right?" they asked together. I rolled my sock down to look at my ankle. It was starting to swell up.

"Maybe it's broken," I moaned.

Source: Sparklers, *The Zipper*, Blake Education. [abridged]

What did Nathan actually do? How do you know?

____

____

____

"The x-ray showed nothing broken. But the doctor said it's a very nasty sprain," Dad said. "Why did you do a stupid thing like jumping off a roof?" he asked.

"I didn't want Owen and Nick to think I was ..."

Source: Sparklers, *The Zipper*, Blake Education. [abridged]

Shade the thought bubble that shows what Nathan was thinking.

a) "I didn't want my friends to think I was scared."

b) "I didn't want my friends to think my Superman cape was fake."

c) "I didn't want my friends to think I didn't want to watch TV with them."

You've heard of a green thumb, but how about a green claw? Decorator crabs love gardens so much that they plant them on their bodies! They use their flexible (bendy) claws to attach sponges to the special Velcro-type bristles on their shells. The sponges continue to grow while on the crab's back.

Source: *That's Bizarre*, Pascal Press.

PREDICTING

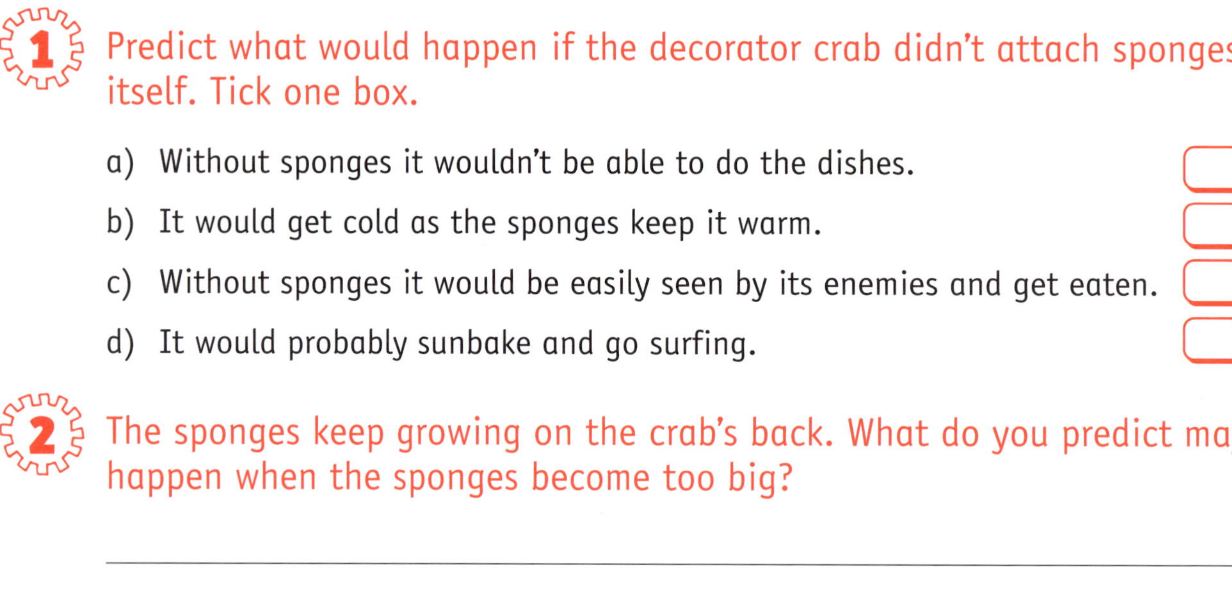

1 Predict what would happen if the decorator crab didn't attach sponges to itself. Tick one box.

a) Without sponges it wouldn't be able to do the dishes. ☐

b) It would get cold as the sponges keep it warm. ☐

c) Without sponges it would be easily seen by its enemies and get eaten. ☐

d) It would probably sunbake and go surfing. ☐

2 The sponges keep growing on the crab's back. What do you predict may happen when the sponges become too big?

____

____

3 Decorator crabs have flexible claws. What might happen if their claws weren't bendy? Colour one flexible arrow.

a) The crab may not be able to do all its exercises very well.	
b) The crab wouldn't be able to scratch its own back very well.	
c) Not every part of the crab's back would be covered, so it may be seen more easily.	

TARGETING COMPREHENSION 3 © PASCAL PRESS ISBN 9781925490626

'Tongues with tentacles' (octopus arms) sounds like the title of a horror movie! But these animals are real — and may even be out in your backyard! Rainbow lorikeets feed on pollen and nectar. Their tongues have tiny tentacles to help them out, just like sea anemones.

Source: *That's Bizarre*, Pascal Press.

PREDICTING

4 Why do rainbow lorikeets have a tongue like this? What could it make them better at?

____

____

____

Another bird has a tongue which is adapted (made) to help it get the food it needs. This bird has a tongue almost as long as itself. It needs this because ____________. It is the hummingbird which is very small and also lives off nectar.

Source: *That's Bizarre*, Pascal Press.

5 Why does the hummingbird have such a long, thin tongue? Tick the box that best explains why.

a) The flowers try to make it hard for the birds to get lots of nectar. ☐

b) Hummingbirds wouldn't be able to hum without their long tongue. ☐

c) Hummingbirds are only small so they need a long tongue to help them fly. ☐

d) Their long tongue helps them get nectar from very long, thin flowers. ☐

6 Predict what would happen if the hummingbird's tongue was only half as long.

____

____

____

PREDICTING

Are you poor? Are you hungry? No? Well, there are hundreds of thousands of children who don't have enough to eat and can't afford to go to school. We can make a difference by raising money through the *Bag a Book* Campaign.

The campaign begins on February 1. All you have to do is fill a bag with books your family no longer wants and bring it to school. It doesn't matter if you bring only one book, it will make a difference to someone, somewhere.

The books will be sold at a *Bag a Bargain Book Sale* in the Assembly Hall on April 1 and 2.

Let's get other kids involved. Phone your friends or email them. Ask them to drop books off at your house or at your school.

Remember, every book you bring will help a child in need. The money we raise from the book sale will buy food, clothing, clean drinking water as well as paper, pencils and books.

Come on! Let's all work together to make this campaign a huge success!

How can bringing books to school help a child in need? Colour any boxes that apply.

a) They will help children to read better. ☐

b) They will make children go to school. ☐

c) They will be sold to raise money for children in need. ☐

d) Money from the book sale will help feed and clothe poor children. ☐

Persuasive Text

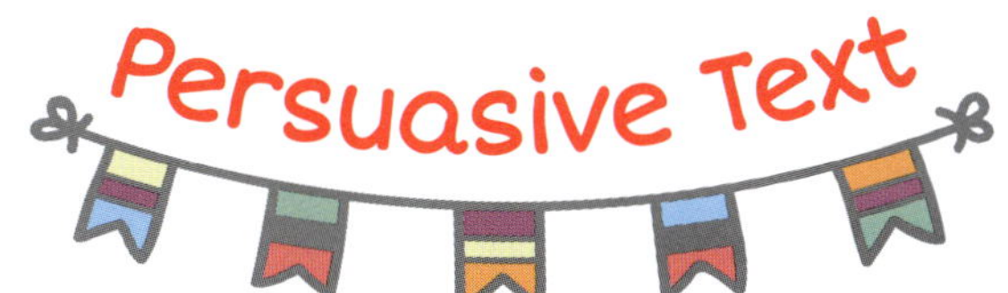

2 How long is the *Bag a Book* Campaign? Tick the correct answer.

a) three weeks
b) six weeks
c) two months
d) a fortnight

3 Write a title for this text.

____

4 If you were a child in need, how would this campaign help you? Colour any that apply.

a) It would provide the money to buy me food, clothes, water and things for school.

b) It would give me lots of books to read.

c) It would help me learn so I can grow up to get a job and buy the things I need.

d) It would make me happy to be able to go to school with my friends.

5 Colour the box that best explains why we need clean water to drink.

a) It tastes good.
b) It is free from diseases that make us ill.
c) It is better than sea water.
d) It is cheaper than soft drink.

PREDICTING

Quick Guide to:

ANALYSING

Humans are dopey creatures. They think that they own the planet or something. This is really silly because everyone in the ocean knows that the owners are the whales and dolphins.

Whales and dolphins are never going to destroy the oceans and all the creatures in them. They have too much respect for that to happen. Whales know that without clean oceans the world may be in very big trouble.

Humans throw rubbish into the water, hunt and kill too many fish, and spread their poisons everywhere. Humans, dolphins and whales need clean air to survive, but even this is being messed up. Sea plants and creatures are slowly starting to die and this may be what happens to all creatures on Earth.

Answering questions about text often means finding the answer in what you have read. Sometimes you are asked to remember what was in the text. These are **literal** questions.

Example of a literal question:
What is one way humans are putting our sea creatures in danger?

Answer: Humans are putting rubbish into the ocean and this is poisoning the water.

Unlike literal questions, when you **analyse**, the answer is not in the text. **Analysing** is reading and thinking about all the information and guessing what idea this is giving to readers.

Example of an analysing question:
What is the difference between whales, dolphins and humans in the way they treat the oceans?

Answer: Whales and dolphins respect the oceans but humans don't care and may end up destroying all life.

DID YOU NOTICE?

When you **analyse** text, you have to read carefully and use the information to make up your mind about **what is really meant**. When you infer and predict, you also have to do this. Analysing means that all of the text needs to be thought about.

"Toby, are you sure you'll be alright sleeping out here?" asked Grandma as she tucked him into the big bed in the back room. "Wouldn't you be more comfortable in the room you normally sleep in when you stay over?"

"Oh, don't worry, Gran," said Toby's sister Olivia, who was sitting on a chair next to the bed. "Toby won't be sleeping here all night. Just keep the hallway light on so he can make his way back to the other room."

Gran gave Toby a kiss before she left. "Remember, I am just down the hall."

Source: Gigglers, *The Heebie Jeebie*, Blake Education. [abridged]

ANALYSING

1 What do you think Grandma is like with her grandchildren? Tick the box that best tells about her.

a) Grandma was not all that worried about Toby. ☐

b) Grandma knew she would be woken and didn't want that. ☐

c) Grandma was interested in watching TV and couldn't be bothered. ☐

d) Grandma was caring and worried about her grandchildren. ☐

2 Write down a sentence from the text above which shows Grandma's feelings for Toby.

____

____

3 Colour the block which you think might happen in the story.

Statement	Block
a) Toby is too frightened to sleep in the big bed all night.	
b) Grandma throws a party with loud music and lots of people.	
c) Toby cries like a little baby.	
d) Toby is brave and sleeps in the big bed all night.	

ANALYSING

"Just remember, they can smell your fear," said Olivia when Gran had gone. "And whatever you do, don't scream. It only gets them more excited."

"Will you stop trying to freak me out!" cried Toby.

Source: Gigglers, *The Heebie Jeebie*, Blake Education. [abridged]

4 Toby's big sister was trying to scare him. What sort of person do you think she is after reading this text?

____

____

____

The scratching sound came from behind the curtains. Toby began to tremble. He held Batbat (teddy) close and wrapped himself as tight as he could in the smell of lavender and mothballs. Suddenly, there was a fast pitter-patter across the floor. It stopped under the bed. Toby heard what he thought was hissing. Without any warning, he leapt out of bed, switched on the light and stood in the middle of the room.

Source: Gigglers, *The Heebie Jeebie*, Blake Education. [abridged]

5 Strange noises in the night had woken Toby. Which one of the statements below best describes what Toby did?

a) Toby was frightened and just wanted to go back to sleep. ☐

b) Although Toby was scared, he got out of bed. This shows how brave he was. ☐

c) Toby didn't think about the sounds because he thought he was dreaming. ☐

d) Toby got out of bed to protect Batbat. ☐

6 Circle the shape which best suits the story.
Toby wrapped himself and held Batbat close. He did this because …

... he was cold and wanted to be warm.	... he wanted to make sure Batbat was safe.	... he wanted to feel safe and secure.

TARGETING COMPREHENSION 3 © PASCAL PRESS ISBN 9781925490626

Over the last two decades (20 years), there have been over 200 shark attacks in Australia. More than half of these attacks occurred in the last decade (10 years). Are sharks becoming more violent? Or are we just getting in their way more? Of the 170 species (types) of sharks in Australian waters, only three types are people killers: the bull shark, tiger shark and great white shark.

Source: *That's Lethal*, Pascal Press. [abridged]

Read these statements. Tick the box of the most correct statement.

a) Sharks are dangerous animals — more attacks means more sharks. ☐

b) Sharks in Australian waters are dangerous, but most people don't care. ☐

c) There are more shark attacks, but not all sharks attack humans. ☐

d) A shark's favourite food is humans who wear sunscreen. ☐

ANALYSING

What could you say to someone who is worried about getting attacked by a shark while swimming at the beach?

____

____

What does the writer mean by, "Are we just getting in the way more?" Shade the best statement.

a) Bull, tiger and great white sharks are very hungry for humans.

b) There are more people in the water every year so there are more shark attacks.

c) Sharks are really not worth worrying about because there are more people for them to eat.

After being bitten once, most people taken by sharks are released. Maybe the shark mistook a human for its usual prey. The shark may be backing off when it realises the flavour's all wrong — perhaps sharks don't find us too tasty! Around 30 percent of all recorded attacks don't result in any injury to the victim.

Shark attacks aren't always fatal, and many victims survive. Bethany Hamilton, an American surfer, lost her arm when attacked. She continues to surf — and even still competes!

Source: *That's Lethal*, Pascal Press. [abridged]

ANALYSING

4 Write the ending in the box that best explains about shark attacks.

Sharks may attack and then leave people because ...

a) quite often they are too lazy to eat any more.

b) they would prefer to eat fish or seals.

c) they would prefer to chase their prey.

5 What is the main idea of this text? Is it about the brave surfer or is it about sharks not attacking humans on purpose?

6 Why does the writer tell us about Bethany Hamilton? Colour the block of the best statement.

a) This surfer didn't blame the shark and kept up with her sport.

b) The surfer was silly because she had already been bitten.

c) She was very brave but should never get back into the water.

d) She got lucky when she was bitten and shouldn't be scared.

TARGETING COMPREHENSION 3 © PASCAL PRESS ISBN 9781925490626

Targeting Comprehension
Year 3 Answers

Literal

Page 2

1 b
2 lay, surfed, jumped, tumbled, grabbed
3 a – 3, b – 2, c – 4, d – 1
4 False
5 ***Sample answer*** Harper tumbled about under the water; scrambled for the surface; grabbed her surfboard; draped her arms over the board and floated; caught her breath; shook salt out of her eyes; set her jaw and decided to try again.
6 jaw, eyes, sure

Page 4

1 False
2 c
3 spins, rotating, axis
4 one day/24 hours
5 Because the Earth rotates, we can't always see the sun from where we are.
6 answers will vary

Page 6

1 c
2 almost 3000 times
3 27
4 True
5 experiment, invention, Thomas Edison; practice, sport, Michael Jordan; ask, book, Dr Seuss
6 ***Sample answer*** We will only achieve our goal if we keep trying.

Inferring

Page 9

1 ***Sample answer*** It was bad weather for sailing because they were in a storm with lightning, wind and rain.
2 a
3 b
4 ***Sample answer*** The deck was slippery. / They might hit the rocks. / The waves were big.
5 rain, wind, waves
6 c

Page 11

1 c
2 ***Sample answer*** Jellyfish look like plastic bags because they are clear and they float.
3 b
4 ***Sample answer*** The gecko's tail may look like a leaf or some bark to blend in or disguise itself.
5 a
6 ***Sample answer*** These geckos have claws to climb trees and rocks.

Page 13

1 c
2 ***Sample answer*** Pitcher plants eat insects.
3 ***Sample answer*** The persuasive text is trying to encourage you to buy a pitcher plant.
4 b

Predicting

Page 16

1 b
2 ***Sample answer*** The boys had been playing so maybe Nathan had to get a ball off the roof.
3 ***Sample answer*** It's summer so maybe the boys had been playing cricket.
4 c
5 ***Sample answer*** Nathan jumped off the roof. His ankle was swelling and he thought it might be broken.
6 a

Page 18

1 c
2 ***Sample answer*** When the sponges become too big, the crab rips them off as they're also heavy.
3 c
4 ***Sample answer*** Rainbow lorikeets have a tongue with tentacles so that plenty of food sticks to their tongue.
5 d
6 ***Sample answer*** They wouldn't be able to get nectar from very long flowers. They would have to feed from shorter flowers.

Page 20

1 c, d
2 c
3 ***Sample answer*** The Bag a Book Campaign
4 a, c, d
5 b

Analysing

Page 23

1 d
2 Gran gave Toby a kiss before she left. / She tucked him into the big bed.
3 d
4 ***Sample answer*** Olivia is mean and nasty for teasing Toby.
5 b
6 … he wanted to feel safe and secure.

Page 25

1 c
2 ***Sample answer*** Not all sharks are man-eaters. / Many people swim at the beach but not many get attacked. / We need to stay out of their way by swimming in safe areas.
3 b
4 b
5 This text is about sharks not attacking people on purpose.
6 a

Page 27

1 d
2 ***Sample answer*** You may die if you can't swallow or breathe.
3 c
4 ***Sample answers***
Laughing makes the muscles in your neck grow which can eventually lead to death.
Smiling can make you ugly and blind.
These are silly ideas because they're not true at all.
5 a, c, e, f

TARGETING COMPREHENSION 3 © PASCAL PRESS ISBN 9781925490626

Making Connections

Page 30

1 b
2 ***Sample answer*** Giant Jim looked huge and powerful and it was a dangerous situation for Sam to be in.
3 b, c
4 Sam felt relaxed, safe and comfortable in his bed.

Page 32

1 b, d
2 ***Sample answer*** Whales and dolphins are like dugongs because they are mammals, they breathe air and feed their young on milk.
3 a
4 ***Sample answer*** The trapdoor spider's lid stops predators from entering just like a plug stops water from flowing down a drain.
5 d
6 answers will vary

Page 34

1 d
2 crazy, dangerous, risk, death, banned, killed
3 Persuasive text (stars): a, b, e
Information text (circles): c, d
4 a

Critical Reflection

Page 37

1 ***Sample answer*** Sarah may have been feeling upset, mad, disappointed, cranky, etc.
2 b
3 ***Sample answer*** Sarah is upset that she wasn't invited so she is pretending she doesn't want to go to the party.
4 b
5 c

Page 39

1 a – 4, b – 2, c – 3, d – 1
2 ***Sample answer*** There would be more snake bites in the country because more snakes live in the country. There is more bushland, grass, farms etc.
3 c, e
4 ***Sample answers*** Step away from the snake. / Don't threaten it. / Keep an eye on the snake. / Yell out for help.
5 b, d, e

Page 41

1 brave, strong, trusting; b,d
2 answers will vary
3 a – 1st, b – 1st, c – 2nd, d – 2nd
4 Even though there is danger, each climber is safe and reaches the top.
5 b, d

Assessment

Page 43

1 lettuce, capsicum, cucumber
2 to protect your hands
3 False
4 a, d
5 c
6 seeds, pot, soil, plants, holes

Page 45

1 a – 3, b – 1, c – 2, d – 4
2 plants, oxygen, healthy
3 b
4 a
5 True
6 c

Page 47

1 ***Sample answer*** They are tall / can weigh as much as a person / jump higher than a tall person / move as fast as a car / carry babies in a pouch / sometimes fight to see who's the strongest / are on our country's crest.
2 tall, weigh, person
3 True
4 b
5 b
6 strong, powerful, large, social, quick

Page 49

1 b
2 A lot – it would make a big difference.
3 ***Sample answer*** No, because Avery prepared for the race, she has determination and she is a positive thinker.
4 ***Sample answer*** Avery will join Cameron's Little Athletics group, get help with her running and improve her ability to run quickly.
5 d

Page 51

1 ***Sample answer*** They are good companions, helpful, understanding and caring.
2 ***Sample answer*** to convince people that dogs are good pets
3 a, c
4 a, b
5 a) Fact
b) Opinion
6 ***Sample answer*** Yes, the author only gives positive examples about dogs.

Page 53

1 a – 4, b – 2, c – 1, d – 3
2 ***Sample answer*** Mike has to do a project but thinks it will be boring. Grandma helps him find a way to make it more interesting.
3 answers will vary
4 answers will vary
5 answers will vary
6 answers will vary

Page 55

1 angry
2 ***Sample answer*** Yes, because he was angry that Ryan ate his cake and cake is tasty.
3 ***Sample answer*** Yes, she was watching eagerly and smiling.
4 ***Sample answer*** Yes, because it was exactly what he'd asked for; there were a lot of pencils; there were a lot of colours and shades.

TARGETING COMPREHENSION 3 © PASCAL PRESS ISBN 9781925490626

Laugh and it may be the last thing you do! Twed Teedybunk, a scientist, has found that laughing is bad for you. Laughing makes the muscles in your neck grow in size and this can make it hard for you to swallow. "No swallowing, no breathing and we all know what happens next!" Twed told other scientists a few days ago.

Mr Teedybunk also spoke about other problems with laughing. Laughing may mean that you are too happy! Being happy all the time can give you smiling wrinkles — very ugly as you get older. Some people who smile too much find that their eyes become narrow slits, perhaps leading to becoming blind.

Smiling and laughing are nothing to be happy about! Think about that next grin! Smiling can make you ugly and blind!

ANALYSING

Of course, what is written here is not really the truth. It is written as persuasive text. Supporting ideas help to make text more persuasive. They give extra information.

1 What do the supporting ideas in the story say? Tick the best sentence.

The supporting details say that …

a) smiling is bad for you because you can be too happy. ☐

b) laughing is good for you and everyone should have a good old laugh. ☐

c) scientists have too much time on their hands and should get a life! ☐

d) smiling can make you blind, can cause wrinkles as you age and can affect your breathing. ☐

2 The scientist says that 'we all know what happens next'. What would happen next if he is right?

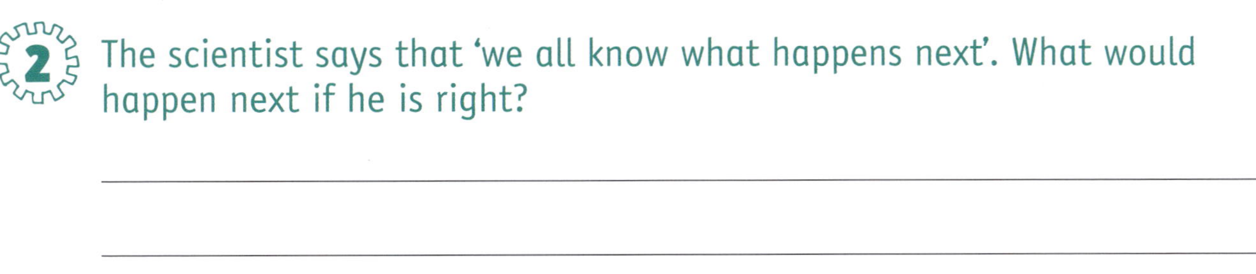

3 What is Twed Teedybunk saying may happen if we laugh too much? Colour the star of the best statement.

a) Laughing can make you breathe faster.	☆
b) Laughing can help you live longer.	☆
c) Laughing can make the muscles in your neck larger.	☆
d) Laughing is not anything to smile about.	☆
e) Laughing is good for you because it can make you blind.	☆

ANALYSING

4 Write **one** idea from the text that is a supporting idea but is not sensible. Write why you think it is silly.

____

____

____

5 The boxes on the left have sentences that are **not true**. Shade four boxes (sentences a to f) which have **true** statements about laughing.

Being happy all the time can give you smiling wrinkles. These are ugly when you are older.	a) Smiling makes a person look friendlier.
	b) Being sad all the time is much better for your skin.
	c) Wrinkles happen when skin becomes older.
People who smile too much find that their eyes become narrow. This may blind them.	d) Your eyelids become fatter when you laugh too much.
	e) Doctors say people who smile and laugh are healthier.
	f) Smiling does not make you go blind.

TARGETING COMPREHENSION 3 © PASCAL PRESS ISBN 9781925490626

Quick Guide to:

• MAKING CONNECTIONS •

There is an old joke that says, "A sea turtle is so slow it gets lost going around in a circle". This could be true because they really are that slow.

For a really boring creature which everyone thought was not all that brainy, Ted was really quite a good thinker. He was the only turtle in the sea that worried about the number of small turtles that weren't showing up out in the ocean after the hatching season.

Ted had watched the sea birds, lizards and humans steal from the nests made by mother turtles. He had tried to tell all the other turtles and sea creatures about this, but they kept falling asleep and snoring so loudly that they never actually heard what he was saying.

Answering questions about text often means finding the answer in what you have read. Sometimes you are asked to remember what was in the text. These are **literal** questions.

Example of a literal question:
What happened when Ted tried to tell the other turtles about the stolen eggs?

Answer: They kept falling asleep and didn't hear what he was saying.

Making connections starts with reading and thinking about all the text. These questions ask you to think about why things in the text are linked or have an effect on another piece of text. **Making connections** asks you to think how two or more different things or actions affect each other.

Example of a making connections question:
Why was the number of small turtles decreasing?

Answer: Sea birds, lizards and humans were stealing the eggs, so the turtles weren't being hatched.

DID YOU NOTICE?

Making connections means thinking about two things in the story and working out **how these are linked** or connected. In the answer above, the sea turtle wasn't listened to or thought of as a good thinker. This happens because he was slow and the other turtles and sea creatures went to sleep. This is not because of what he had to say.

Sam punched the cushion again. Was he kidding? Cleaning your room was more boring than ironing underwear. It was more boring than picking fluff off your jumper with tweezers. "Yeah, later," said Sam. Like next year, he thought.

Source: Gigglers, *Something's Fishy*, Blake Education.

Tick the box of the statement which matches what Sam had really thought when told to clean his room.

a) Sam really just wanted to iron his underwear. ☐

b) Sam thought he would do the cleaning, but a bit later. ☐

c) Sam loves cleaning but just doesn't want to clean his own room. ☐

d) Sam looked forward to cleaning his room. ☐

A giant goldfish appeared in front of Sam, granting him his wish of the most unboring day ever. Fish Face used magic to take Sam to a judo match. Sam listened to the voice on the loudspeaker.

"Round Two. Sam versus Giant Jim."

Sam looked across the mat and saw Giant Jim facing him, waving his huge arms in the air. "Oh my gosh," said Sam. "No way."

Giant Jim bounded towards Sam like a grizzly bear.

Source: Gigglers, *Something's Fishy*, Blake Education. [abridged]

The writer wants to give you an idea of how Giant Jim looked to Sam. This is a simile, where two things are compared because they have similar qualities.

What do you think the writer was trying to say about Giant Jim? Use some of the words below to write a sentence about what was meant.

huge | dangerous | silly | clever | fast

growling | powerful | strange | funny

____

____

____

TARGETING COMPREHENSION 3 © PASCAL PRESS ISBN 9781925490626

"Waterfall!" screamed Sam.

"Yes, I know," said Fish Face. He stood up in the boat like a surfer riding a wave. "I do hope you enjoy your swim," he said. Then he winked at Sam and leapt towards the bank like a flying fish.

Source: GiggLers, *Something's Fishy*, Blake Education.

The writer has included two similes in this text. What is the writer trying to make readers think? Shade two phrases which explain how Fish Face moved.

a) looked wobbly on the water	b) skimmed quickly over the water
c) was really well balanced	d) fell into the water
e) was frightened and jumped	f) was out of control standing up in the boat
g) felt nervous leaping towards the bank	h) jumped clumsily to the bank

The soft blankets soothed him like a warm bath. His pillow felt as soft as a marshmallow. Sam relaxed and soon he was in a deep sleep.

Source: GiggLers, *Something's Fishy*, Blake Education.

By using similes, the writer is trying to make the reader think something about the way Sam felt. Colour the shape that is the best fit.

Sam was tired but he was still hungry and was dreaming of marshmallows.

Sam enjoyed getting into bed as he thought his father may bring him some marshmallows.

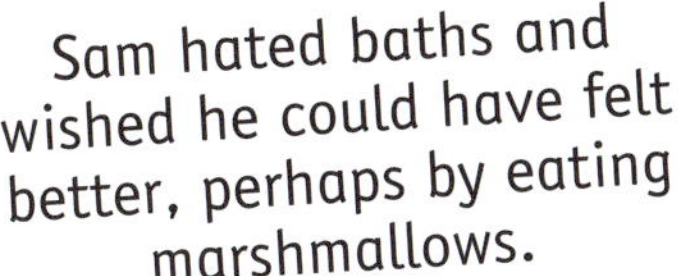

Sam hated baths and wished he could have felt better, perhaps by eating marshmallows.

Sam felt relaxed, safe and comfortable in his bed.

It's said that dugongs used to be mistaken for mermaids (half fish and half woman). Dugongs are far from the graceful sirens (mermaids) of the sea found in myths (stories). They can grow to 3 metres long and weigh over 400 kilograms. Dugongs even have bristles on their upper lips, rather like moustaches!

Source: *That's Bizarre*, Pascal Press. [abridged]

Dugongs are not like mermaids who are half woman and half fish. Tick two correct statements.

Dugongs are definitely **not** like mermaids because …

a) they are all male. ☐

b) they are very large and heavy. ☐

c) mermaids don't like dugongs much. ☐

d) they are very long and have bristles. ☐

MAKING CONNECTIONS

Dugongs are mammals, they breathe air and feed their young on milk. Can you name another ocean mammal and say how it is the same as the dugong?

____

____

____

Some spiders make parachutes from their bottoms to form a balloon. They point their bottoms skywards and shoot out silk. The spider then waits for a breeze to catch it and carry them away.

Source: *That's Bizarre*, Pascal Press. [abridged]

Choose the best ending to the statement and shade it.

The writer compares the web of the spider with a parachute because …	
	a) the web allows them to float using the breeze to move.
	b) the web they make is round and stretchy like rubber.
	c) the web stops them from crashing into things.

TARGETING COMPREHENSION 3 © PASCAL PRESS ISBN 9781925490626

The trapdoor spider makes a special tight-fitting lid for its hole, rather like a bath plug. If predators (animals that eat it) come knocking, the spider can hold the door shut with its claws.

Source: *That's Bizarre*, Pascal Press. [abridged]

4 The writer has said that the trapdoor spider lid is like a plug in a bath. How is the spider's trapdoor similar to a bath plug?

____

____

____

5 The statements below compare the trapdoor lid and a door. One word from the text makes the lid and the door sound similar. Colour the star of the best comparison.

The writer ...

a) compares the lid with the door because they both have a tight fit. ☆

b) says the lid and the door are made of wood. ☆

c) says the lid and the door are the same colour. ☆

d) uses the word 'knocking' which is something that happens with doors. ☆

MAKING CONNECTIONS

Pelicans have massive bills. In fact, the Australian pelican has the longest bill of any bird! Its pouch can hold 13 litres of water. That's 13 cartons of milk!

Source: *That's Bizarre*, Pascal Press.

6 Think of something that carries things that you could compare with that giant beak. Explain how your choice is like the pelican's beak.

____

____

____

____

New Zealander A. J. Hackett bungeed 324 metres from the Eiffel Tower (a really tall tower in Paris, France) in 1987. He opened the world's first commercial (people pay money) bungee jump in New Zealand the following year. Now many people free-fall about 50 metres for a thrill they don't forget quickly!

Source: Brainwaves, *To the Limit*, Blake Education. [abridged]

Read the text below. This gives the same story but has been written persuasively.

Would you jump off the Eiffel Tower strapped only to a long, elastic cord? That's exactly what A. J. Hackett did in 1987, grabbing world-wide attention for this crazy, dangerous sport, which he called Bungee Jumping.

One year later, he opened the world's first commercial Bungee Jump. Why would you pay to jump off bridges and buildings? What if the bungee cord was too long, or it broke? The risk of death is too high. Surely this is a sport that should be banned before people get killed.

Both texts give the same information, but one gives the reader a different idea to the other. Tick the box next to the text that finishes the statement best.

One of these texts is …

a) trying to persuade people to take up bungee jumping. ☐

b) trying to give people the idea that bungee jumping is safe and it is now done all over the world. ☐

c) telling about someone who is jealous because they didn't think of the idea. ☐

d) telling where bungee started and who was the first person to start the craze. ☐

TARGETING COMPREHENSION 3 © PASCAL PRESS ISBN 9781925490626

2 The persuasive text is trying to tell people that bungee jumping can be very dangerous. Write as many words as you can find in the text that tell us it is dangerous.

____

____

____

____

3 Read the statements and colour a **star** if it is from the **persuasive** text and colour a **circle** if it is from the **information** text.

a) Why would you pay to jump off bridges …	☆	○
b) This sport should be banned.	☆	○
c) Many people freefall about 50 metres.	☆	○
d) He bungeed 324 metres from the Eiffel Tower.	☆	○
e) The risk of death is too high.	☆	○

4 How did the writer make this sport sound dangerous? Colour the block next to the best answer.

a) By saying the sport was crazy and dangerous. ▢

b) By being fair and saying that this sport could be dangerous. ▢

c) By looking at the sport and picking out the best bits to persuade people to have a go. ▢

d) By telling readers how enjoyable bungee jumping can be. ▢

MAKING CONNECTIONS

Quick Guide to:

• CRITICAL REFLECTION •

Humans throw plenty of rubbish into the water, but blue plastic strapping from bait boxes is the worst. These are circles of death which dolphins and other sea animals think are playthings. Made of tough plastic, these strangle or cut to the bone once around the animal. Creatures suffer an agonising death.

Roger the crocodile had become a hero. Yes, this scaly, toothy and evil-looking creature was famous amongst sea creatures. Roger had learned to chase any sea creature he saw caught in a blue strap. Swimming up behind them, he'd snap the plastic with his powerful jaws. Animals who hadn't heard about Roger were more than worried when he swam toward them ...

Answering questions about text often means finding the answer in what you have read. Sometimes you are asked to remember what was in the text. These are **literal** questions.

Example of a literal question:
What did Roger do to help other sea creatures?

Answer: Roger would help animals by chasing them and biting through the plastic straps.

Critical reflection starts with reading and thinking about all the text. These questions ask you to think about how things happen, how they affect what is happening and the feelings of characters.

Example of a critical reflection question:
Creatures who didn't know Roger were worried when he swam towards them. What were they thinking and how would they have felt after being helped?

Answer: Because Roger was a crocodile, they would have been scared of being eaten. After they were helped, they would have been grateful.

DID YOU NOTICE?

The answer is not in the text. You have to **read and decide** how the characters are thinking. You have to read and think about your feelings about a character, or about a topic. You have to **use your ideas** to find the answer by thinking of your experiences.

TARGETING COMPREHENSION 3 © PASCAL PRESS ISBN 9781925490626

Sarah threw her schoolbag onto the floor and slumped into the kitchen with a sigh. "How was school?" asked her dad as he busily chopped vegetables for dinner.

"Mmmhh," grumbled Sarah.

"That good, huh?"

Sarah poured herself a glass of water. "It's just dumb, that's all."

"What's dumb?" he asked, slicing some carrots.

"School," Sarah replied, "... and everyone."

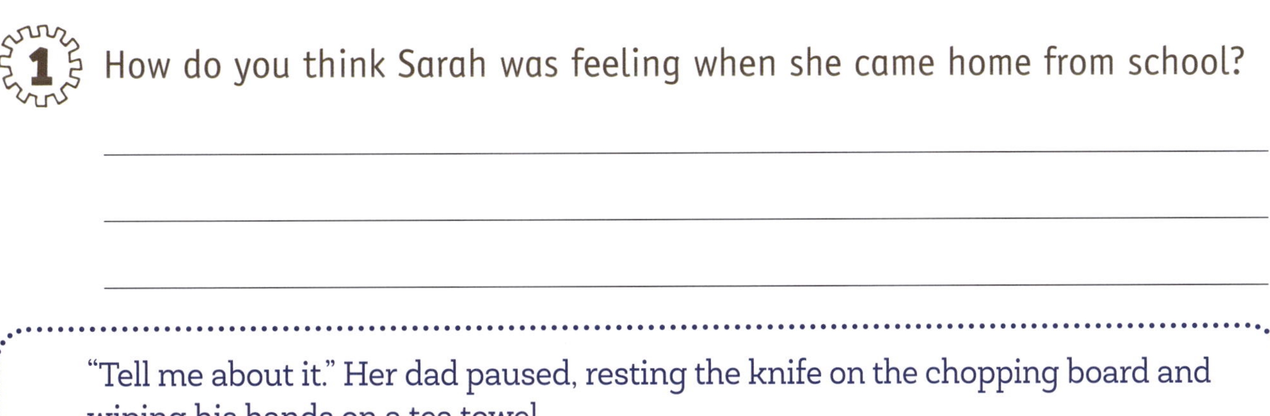

1 How do you think Sarah was feeling when she came home from school?

"Tell me about it." Her dad paused, resting the knife on the chopping board and wiping his hands on a tea towel.

"You wouldn't understand," Sarah mumbled.

"Try me," said her dad. "I've been to school — I know a few things."

2 What did Sarah's dad mean when he said he knew a few things? Tick the correct answer.

a) He had learnt a lot of things at school. ☐

b) He would understand what she was talking about. ☐

c) He was very clever and knew lots of facts. ☐

"Elliot gave everyone else an invitation to his birthday party," she began, "but I didn't get one."

"Ah, I see," her dad mused.

"It's dumb. I wouldn't want to go anyway," Sarah scowled.

3 Why was Sarah saying that she wouldn't want to go to the party?

____

____

____

Sarah's dad thought for a moment. "Have you spoken to Elliot about it?" he asked.

"No," Sarah frowned.

"Why not?"

"Elliot wasn't at school today," she explained.

"When were the invitations handed out?" Sarah's dad asked.

"Yesterday," Sarah said, "and it's all anyone can talk about."

4 What does Sarah mean when she says that the party is all anyone can talk about? Tick the correct answer.

a) No-one is allowed to talk about any other topic except the party. ☐

b) Everyone is excited about the party and they are talking about it a lot. ☐

"So ... the invitations were handed out yesterday," her dad confirmed.

"Yes," Sarah replied impatiently.

"And you were away yesterday," her dad continued.

"Yeah."

"Do you think that maybe Elliot has an invitation for you as well but hasn't been able to give it to you yet?" Sarah's dad questioned.

Sarah looked up from the floor. "Hmmm ... maybe," she admitted with a shrug.

5 How would you best label Sarah's reaction to not receiving an invitation? Tick the correct answer.

a) Under-reaction: She didn't really care about the problem. ☐

b) Fair reaction: She reacted about as strongly as she should. ☐

c) Over-reaction: Sarah reacted too strongly to the situation. ☐

TARGETING COMPREHENSION 3 © PASCAL PRESS ISBN 9781925490626

Many snakes kill their food by paralysing it. They inject the prey with venom that contains strong toxins (poisons). The toxin interferes with the victim's nervous system. It can't move, and eventually it stops breathing and dies.

Source: *That's Lethal*, Pascal Press.

1. Below are the steps in treating a snake bite. Put them in order by numbering them. The first step is 1, and 4 is the last step.

   a) Tell the neighbours to watch out for snakes because of this. ☐

   b) Lay the victim down so that their blood flows less quickly. ☐

   c) Wrap the whole arm or leg in a bandage to stop it from moving. ☐

   d) Call the ambulance as quickly as you can. ☐

2. Would there be more snake bites in the city or in the country? Explain why you have made this choice.

   ____

   ____

   ____

3. Snake bites can be deadly. Tick two sentences that you think are correct.

   a) Snakes kill other animals for fun. ☐

   b) The snake's prey can't move after being bitten because it is so scared. ☐

   c) The snake's prey stops breathing because it is paralysed. ☐

   d) The snake's prey dies from fright. ☐

   e) The nervous system controls the animal's movement and breathing. ☐

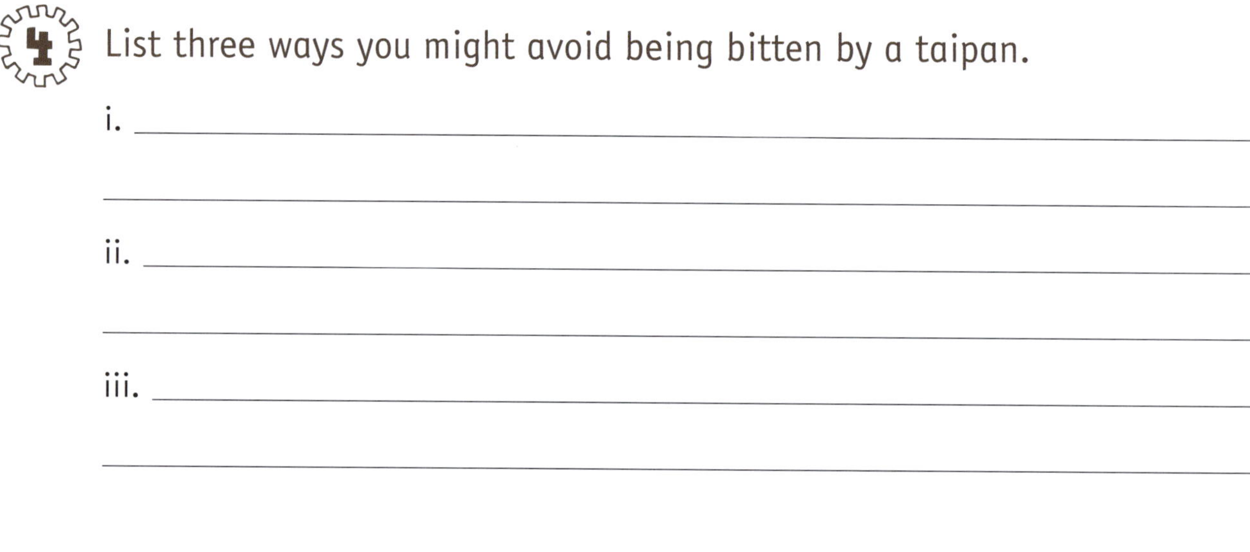

It's official. The taipan has been awarded the 'most dangerous Australian snake' title! Like most snakes, they prefer to slither away unnoticed. But if you corner one and take it by surprise — WHOMP! The taipan won't hesitate. Even the slightest movement can trigger an attack. Taipans hurl themselves into the air and strike so fast that a person can be bitten repeatedly before even noticing the snake is there!

Source: *That's Lethal*, Pascal Press. [abridged]

4 List three ways you might avoid being bitten by a taipan.

i. ______________________________

____

ii. ______________________________

____

iii. ______________________________

____

What would you do if you saw a taipan in your backyard? Colour the blocks of the sentences which are the safe things to do.

a) Try to calm the snake by patting it gently. ☐

b) Step well back from the snake. Don't threaten it in any way. ☐

c) Try to catch the snake if it strikes out at you. ☐

d) Watch the snake. Keep your eyes on the reptile at all times. ☐

e) Call a warning and yell for help. ☐

CRITICAL REFLECTION

1st It is a slow hard climb up the side of a cliff. Teamwork and trust are very important to rock climbers. The first climber up the cliff fixes pegs into cracks in the rocks. Then he or she attaches a rope to metal pegs. Rock climbers have to be very fit and brave because …

Source: Brainwaves, *To the Limit*, Blake Education. [abridged]

Read the text below. This gives the same story but has been written persuasively.

2nd You would have to be crazy to go rock climbing. It's such a dangerous team sport. Not only is it a slow, hard climb to the top, the risk of falling is high. You must trust your leader to fix metal pegs firmly into the rock wall. Remember, you are only attached to these pegs with a rope. If one comes loose, you could slip and fall to your death. Why risk your life for such an extreme sport?

1 In the first text, how does the writer describe rock climbers? Tick the boxes that apply.

- ☐ brave
- ☐ silly
- ☐ strong
- ☐ selfish
- ☐ trusting
- ☐ crazy

In the second text, the writer argues against rock climbing. What are the reasons? Colour the boxes that apply.

a) You have to cling to a rock wall. ☐

b) A metal peg may come loose and you could fall. ☐

c) You can't trust the leader. ☐

d) You have to be crazy to take the risk. ☐

2 Do you think rock climbing should be banned? Give reasons for your opinion.

____

____

____

CRITICAL REFLECTION

Which text does the sentence match? Colour the block of either the 1st or 2nd text.

a) Working well in a team helps in this sport.	1st	2nd
b) They know the danger. Strength is so important.	1st	2nd
c) You would have to be crazy to do this sport.	1st	2nd
d) It's very likely rock climbers would fall to their death.	1st	2nd

Read the text in each of the shapes. Colour the climber's peg which has an end (outcome) that you think both writers would want.

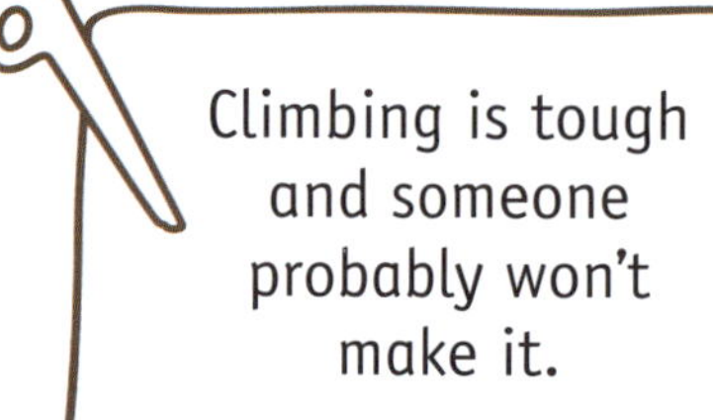

Even though there is danger, each climber is safe and reaches the top.

Rock climbing is not all that hard and everyone should take it up.

In the **2nd** text the writer uses ways of making the reader feel a certain way. Shade two stars that say how the writer wants you to feel.

The feeling the writer wants to create is ...

a) that climbing is not all that scary.	☆
b) that rock climbing is dangerous and any slips could mean death.	☆
c) that if you are fit and strong, it isn't that dangerous.	☆
d) a feeling of danger and that this is not a safe sport in any way.	☆

How to Grow a Salad

It's fun to grow your own food!

What you'll need to get:

- vegetable seeds – lettuce, capsicum, cucumber
- herb seeds – basil, parsley
- gloves
- pots or containers
- soil
- a spade or something to dig with
- a watering can and some water

What you'll need to do:

1. Put on some gloves to protect your hands.
2. Put the soil into the pots or containers.
3. Use the spade to dig small holes for the seeds.
4. Sprinkle the seeds in the holes.
5. Cover the holes with soil.
6. Water the soil so that it is damp.
7. Water the plants regularly and make sure they are placed in the sun.
8. Wait until the plants are ready to pick.
9. Make the tastiest salad you've ever eaten!

1 Tick the vegetables in the salad:

- [ ] basil
- [ ] capsicum
- [ ] lettuce
- [ ] tomato
- [ ] parsley
- [ ] cucumber

ASSESSMENT

2 Why do you need to put gloves on?

____

____

____

3 True or False? You should dig large holes for the seeds.

☐ True ☐ False

4 What should you do to look after the plants? Tick two answers.

a) Water them regularly. ☐
b) Place the plants in the shade. ☐
c) Pick the vegetables. ☐
d) Make sure they are placed in the sun. ☐

5 When should you pick the herbs and vegetables to make the salad? Tick the correct answer.

a) When they are fully grown. ☐
b) When they begin to grow. ☐
c) When they are ready. ☐
d) When you are hungry. ☐

6 Circle the nouns from the text.

sprinkle	dig	seeds	weeds
plants	soil	compost	shade
holes	pot	mulch	shovel

TARGETING COMPREHENSION 3 © PASCAL PRESS ISBN 9781925490626

Looking After a Fish

Fish can be easy pets to keep but you need to do a few things to make sure they stay healthy!

Firstly, you need to make sure the water is just right for the fish. You can't just pour water from the tap and expect it to swim around — you usually need to test the water to make sure it's safe. The pet store might even recommend you put a special chemical in the water to make sure it's safe for your new pet.

Next, place some plants in the water. The plants produce oxygen and help your fish live a healthy, happy life.

Then, you'll need to float the bag containing your fish in the fish tank. You wouldn't want to jump headfirst into freezing water, so let your fish get used to the water temperature in your tank before gently opening the bag so it can swim into the tank.

Lastly, make sure you feed your fish regular, small amounts. Overfeeding your fish can kill it, but make sure it doesn't get too hungry. A small pinch of food a couple of times a day is a good idea.

You'll need to clean the tank regularly, but this is a small price to pay for the beauty of keeping a real, live fish!

There are a few things to do to keep a fish. Number the steps in the right order from 1 to 4.

a) Float the bag in the fish tank. ☐

b) Test the water. ☐

c) Place some plants in the water. ☐

d) Feed your fish small, regular amounts. ☐

ASSESSMENT

2. Next, place some __________ in the water. The plants produce __________ and help your fish live a __________, happy life.

3. Why do you need to test the water? Tick the correct answer.

a) To make sure it's not too hot for the fish. ☐
b) To make sure it's safe for the fish. ☐
c) To make sure it's tasty for the fish. ☐
d) To make sure it's cold enough for the fish. ☐

4. Why do you float the bag containing your fish in the fish tank? Colour the correct answer.

a) Your fish has to get used to the water temperature in the tank. ☐
b) Your fish has to get used to living in a tank instead of a bag. ☐
c) Your fish might get confused when you put it in the tank. ☐
d) Your fish might jump out of the tank when you put it in there. ☐

5. True or False? Overfeeding your fish can kill it.

☐ True ☐ False

6. How often should you feed your fish? Tick the correct answer.

a) once a day ☐
b) once a week ☐
c) a couple of times a day ☐
d) a couple of times a week ☐

TARGETING COMPREHENSION 3 © PASCAL PRESS ISBN 9781925490626

Kangaroos are amazing animals. They look different to most other animals and they can move pretty quickly.

Kangaroos can grow between 1.5 and 2 metres tall. A fully grown male kangaroo can weigh as much as a small person! They have short front legs but it's their powerful back legs and huge feet that help them jump. Kangaroos can jump higher than the height of a really tall person and can move as fast as a car. They use their tail to help them balance.

Female kangaroos have a pouch at the front of their body which is where the joeys or baby kangaroos begin to grow. The tiny newborn joeys get carried around in the pouch until they're old enough to explore safely on their own all the time.

Kangaroos live in many parts of Australia, including rainforests and woodlands. They live in groups called a 'mob'. The mobs have males, females and joeys but the biggest male kangaroo is always the boss of the group. Male kangaroos will sometimes fight to see who's the strongest in the group.

These animals are very special to Australia — they are even on our country's crest. It's great to live in a country that has such amazing animals!

Name three reasons why kangaroos are amazing animals.

____

____

____

ASSESSMENT

2 Kangaroos can grow between 1.5 and 2 metres __________. A fully grown male kangaroo can __________ as much as a small __________!

3 True or False? Kangaroos use their tail to help them balance.

☐ True ☐ False

4 Why would a mother kangaroo carry her joey in its pouch? Tick the correct answer.

a) because the joey would get tired and start whingeing ☐
b) to keep the joey safe ☐
c) so she doesn't lose the joey ☐
d) to keep the joey close to her because she gets lonely ☐

5 Which statement best describes kangaroos? Tick the correct answer.

a) tall Australian animals that eat leaves ☐
b) strong, fast animals that live in groups ☐
c) amazing, powerful animals that have pouches ☐
d) Australian animals with short arms ☐

6 Colour the adjectives that best describe fully grown kangaroos.

☐ beautiful	☐ clever	☐ dangerous
☐ strong	☐ powerful	☐ social
☐ tiny	☐ large	☐ quick

ASSESSMENT

TARGETING COMPREHENSION 3 © PASCAL PRESS ISBN 9781925490626

Avery's legs kept running, her arms pumping by her sides, her lungs on fire. "Come on!" she told herself. "You can keep going." Avery could hear the cheers of the crowd and she didn't want to give up. But then, out of the corner of her eye, she noticed someone closing in on her.

1 What do you think Avery will do next? Tick the correct answer.

a) give up because running is too hard ☐
b) try to run faster to win ☐
c) slow down because she is tired ☐
d) keep running at the same speed ☐

Avery had been training every day for weeks now. For her, this was the most important sporting day of the year — the day she finally got to compete in the 5-kilometre race. Avery had eaten healthy food with lots of energy to help her run and had even made sure that she got lots of sleep so that she could be at her best. But now, Avery was beginning to doubt herself.

2 How much do you think Avery's preparations helped her running? Tick one box.

a) Not at all – it wouldn't make any difference. ☐
b) A little – it wouldn't make much of a difference. ☐
c) A lot – it would make a big difference. ☐

"I won't give up!" she told herself. "I'll run my hardest." Meanwhile, one of the other runners in the race, Cameron, grew steadily closer.

3 Do you think Cameron's efforts will put Avery off and make her give up? Explain why or why not.

____
____
____

ASSESSMENT

As they neared the finish line, Cameron's long legs began to overtake Avery. Try as she might, Avery just couldn't keep up. Feeling defeated, Avery crossed the finish line second with her heart sinking and her legs aching. "Wow," panted Cameron, "that was amazing!"

"I guess you were," Avery admitted.

"No," Cameron corrected, "your running — you were so fast!"

"Not fast enough," Avery said sadly, trying to catch her breath.

"You should join my Little Athletics group," Cameron said encouragingly. "You'd be a great team member to have on board."

"Really?" asked Avery. "I've never had anyone help me with my running before."

"Are you kidding?" puffed Cameron. "Wow, you sure are determined."

"I guess so." Avery wiped the sweat from her forehead.

"Trust me," Cameron replied. "With a little extra help and all that effort, you're going to be even more amazing."

4 What do you think Avery will do now?

____

____

____

"Thanks." Avery managed a weak smile. "I hope I can learn to run as fast as you one day."

"Trust me," Cameron grinned, "you're already well on the way."

How likely do you think it is that Avery and Cameron will become friends? Tick the correct answer.

a) Impossible – they both dislike each other too much to be friends. ☐

b) Unlikely – they are competitors who need to race against each other. ☐

c) Possible – they both like running so they might become friends. ☐

d) Likely – they are already being friendly and both like the same things. ☐

TARGETING COMPREHENSION 3 © PASCAL PRESS ISBN 9781925490626

Dogs – Man's Best Friend

Humans and dogs have lived together for thousands of years. This partnership has been beneficial for those involved for both practical and emotional reasons.

Dogs are faithful companions – they love to stay by your side. Even if your friends can't come over to play or don't want to hang out with you, your dog always will.

Dogs like to help – whether they're rounding up sheep, helping a blind person cross the road, or fetching the newspaper from the front lawn. Dogs can learn to do things that help humans and they like to help the people who care for them.

Dogs understand you – whether you're cross because they pooped on the carpet or you're sad because you've had a bad day at school. Dogs might not always understand why we have these emotions, but they do know how to react when we're feeling certain ways.

Dogs care for us – whether barking to scare away strangers or cuddling to keep us company. If we look after and care for our dogs, they will look after us faithfully forever.

The bond between humans and dogs is special — sometimes they seem to understand us even better than we understand ourselves.

1 What is the writer trying to get us to think about dogs?

____

____

____

2 Why do you think the writer has written this article?

____

____

____

3 Who might find this article most helpful? Tick two boxes.

a) someone thinking about buying a dog ☐

b) someone who really likes dogs a lot ☐

c) a kid trying to convince a parent to let them buy a dog ☐

d) a person who is very scared of dogs ☐

4 Where do you think this article might be published? Tick two answers.

a) in a magazine about pets ☐

b) on a website for kids ☐

c) in a newspaper ☐

d) in a story book ☐

5 Fact or Opinion? Write which statement is Fact and which is Opinion.

a) Dogs and humans have lived together for thousands of years.

____

b) Dogs make really good pets. __________

6 Do you think the author likes dogs? What makes you say that?

____

____

____

____

TARGETING COMPREHENSION 3 © PASCAL PRESS ISBN 9781925490626

"Ugh," Mike groaned as he walked through the back door.

"Oh dear," his grandma commented, "that doesn't sound good."

"It's not," continued Mike, "it's the worst."

"That bad, hey?" Grandma asked. "Sounds like you'd better sit down and have a glass of milk."

Mike dragged his feet through the kitchen and dumped his school bag on the floor.

His grandma reached into the fridge and then poured a tall glass of cold milk.

"Thanks." Mike took a long gulp, leaving a milk moustache on his top lip.

"So, what's so terrible that you've come home in such a bad mood?" Grandma asked.

"I have to do a project about a country," Mike explained.

"Well that doesn't sound so bad," said Grandma, putting the milk back in the fridge.

"But I have to do the project for homework," groaned Mike.

"Hmm ..." Grandma paused. "How about you pick a country that interests you?"

"Countries are boring," he said, drinking some more milk.

"Well, what about soccer?" asked Grandma.

"Soccer isn't a country, Grandma." Mike rolled his eyes.

"No, but you like soccer, don't you?"

Mike nodded as he took another sip.

"Well, England made soccer really popular. Maybe you could do your project on England."

Mike thought for a moment. "I could write about the famous stadiums and players as part of my project."

"I don't see why not," his grandma said, smiling.

"Thanks, Grandma!" Mike gave her a big hug. "Maybe it won't be so bad after all!"

Place the story events in the correct order. Number the boxes from 1 to 4.

a) Grandma suggested Mike complete the project about England. ☐

b) Grandma poured Mike some milk. ☐

c) Mike came home. ☐

d) Mike complained about his project. ☐

ASSESSMENT

2 What is the main idea in the text? What is this story mostly about?

3 Have you ever asked a grownup for help with a project or homework task?

☐ Yes ☐ No

4 Describe a time when you didn't want to do something but then you realised it wasn't so bad.

5 Describe how Mike's reaction to his project is similar or different to your feelings about a past project or homework task.

6 Explain how this text is similar or different to a book or a movie that you have read or seen.

ASSESSMENT

TARGETING COMPREHENSION 3 © PASCAL PRESS ISBN 9781925490626

"Happy birthday, dear Brodie … Happy birthday to you." The tune was still ringing in his ears as Brodie grinned and leaned forward to blow out his candles.

"Me do!" Suddenly, Ryan leaned toward the cake and began to blow, spit landing all over the bright red icing.

"Ryan!" yelled Brodie. "It's *my* birthday!"

"Ryan doesn't understand, dear," his mother soothed. "He's only two."

"But it's *my birthday!*" Brodie repeated.

1 How do you think Brodie is feeling about Ryan blowing out the candles? Tick your answer.

- ☐ happy
- ☐ angry
- ☐ calm
- ☐ surprised
- ☐ sad
- ☐ afraid
- ☐ joyful
- ☐ pleased
- ☐ grateful

Brodie stared at his spit-covered slice of cake.

"Num nums," Ryan said, red icing dribbling down his chin.

"How about you get your presents and unwrap them?" his mum suggested.

Brodie left his piece of cake at the table and went to fetch his presents.

"Num nums," Ryan repeated, his little hand grasping Brodie's slice of cake.

Brodie turned around. "Ryan!" he yelled. "That was *my* piece of cake."

"There's more cake, dear," his mother said, smiling. "I'll cut you another slice."

2 Do you think Brodie wants to eat the cake? What makes you say that?

☐ Yes ☐ No

____

____

____

ASSESSMENT

Brodie turned his attention to the first shiny present in front of him. He'd asked for a new set of drawing pencils for his birthday, but he couldn't tell what was in the wrapping. His mum stood by, hands clasped to her chin, watching Brodie eagerly with a smile on her face. Brodie tore the wrapping paper eagerly and discovered that he had a sketchpad of high-quality drawing paper.

"Num num", Ryan said, with shiny wrapping sticking out of his mouth.

"Ryan!" Brodie shouted. "Put my present down."

"He doesn't understand, dear," his mum explained.

'But it's *my birthday!*" Brodie exclaimed.

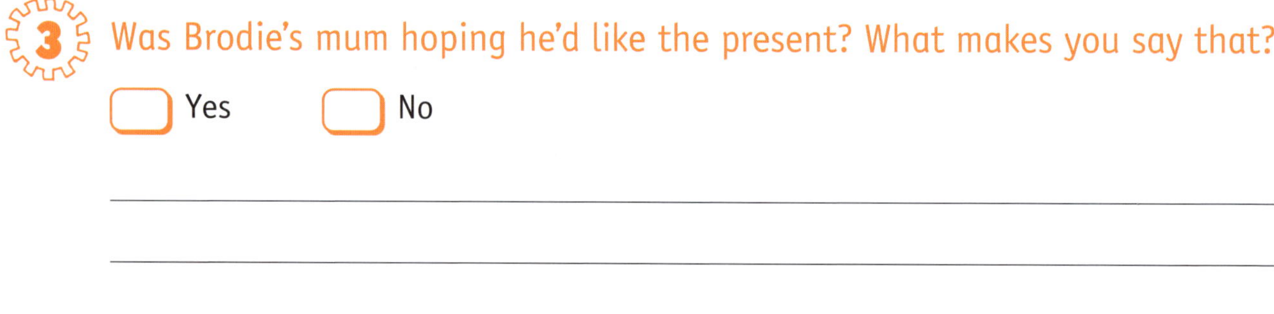

3 Was Brodie's mum hoping he'd like the present? What makes you say that?

☐ Yes ☐ No

"Happy birfday, Bohdee!' Ryan gurgled, holding out the present that had just been in his mouth.

"Thanks, Ryan," Brodie grumbled, taking it from his hands. He began to slowly peel the wet wrapping paper off the box.

"Oh, Mum!" he gasped. "This is exactly what I wanted!" Brodie looked down at the box containing 120 bright, shiny pencils — more colours and shades than you can imagine.

"Ryan helped me choose the present," his mum said.

"Thanks, Ryan," Brodie smiled. "I guess you're not such a bad little brother after all."

4 Does Brodie like his present from Ryan? What makes you say that?

TARGETING COMPREHENSION 3 © PASCAL PRESS ISBN 9781925490626